Hands-On STEM

FOCUS ON MOMENTUM

by Christopher Forest

FOCUS READERS

FOCUS READERS

www.focusreaders.com

Focus Readers is distributed by North Star Editions:
sales@northstareditions.com | 888-417-0195

Produced for Focus Readers by Red Line Editorial.

Content Consultant: Bruce Bolon, Associate Professor of Physics, Hamline University

Photographs ©: ESB Professional/Shutterstock Images, cover, 1; GeorgeManga/iStockphoto, 4–5; stacey_newman/iStockphoto, 7; vitpho/iStockphoto, 8–9; Alija/iStockphoto, 11; scanrail/iStockphoto, 13; vencavolrab/iStockphoto, 15; vuk8691/iStockphoto, 16–17; RobertCrum/iStockphoto, 18; Red Line Editorial, 21, 27; IPGGutenbergUKLtd/iStockphoto, 23; FatCamera/iStockphoto, 25

ISBN
978-1-63517-286-7 (hardcover)
978-1-63517-351-2 (paperback)
978-1-63517-481-6 (ebook pdf)
978-1-63517-416-8 (hosted ebook)

Library of Congress Control Number: 2017935143

Printed in the United States of America
Mankato, MN
June, 2017

About the Author

Christopher Forest is a middle school teacher. In his free time, he enjoys writing books for all ages. He also enjoys watching sports, playing guitar, reading, and spending time outdoors. He lives in Danvers, Massachusetts, with his wife, Melissa, two children, Brighid and Christopher, and his cat, Murray.

TABLE OF CONTENTS

CHAPTER 1

MOMENTUM ON THE PLAYGROUND

Andre is at the playground. He climbs the stairs to the top of the slide. Then, he stands and waits until it is his turn to go down. While Andre is waiting, he is at rest. This means he is not moving.

Slides are fun because of how your momentum changes on the way down.

Finally, it is Andre's turn. He goes down the slide. His body is in **motion**. He goes faster as he moves down the slide.

Momentum is a measurement that tells a lot about an object's motion. Any object that is moving has momentum. On the playground, Andre was moving while he was going down the slide. For this reason, Andre had momentum.

Other playground activities, such as swinging, also involve momentum.

CHAPTER 2

WHAT IS MOMENTUM?

Two things determine an object's momentum. One of these is the object's **velocity**. This describes both the speed of the object and the direction it is moving. For example, think of a large truck.

A truck's velocity changes when it goes around a curve.

On the highway, the truck usually has a high speed. The same truck driving in a parking lot usually has a low speed. The truck has more momentum when it is moving quickly. It has less momentum when it is moving slowly. If the truck is not moving, it has no momentum.

The other thing that affects an object's momentum is its **mass**. Mass is related to the amount and type of material in an object.

These cars are not moving, so they have no momentum.

Imagine that a car and a skateboard are rolling down the street. Suppose they are moving at the same speed. The car has more mass. For this reason, the car has more momentum. The skateboard has less mass. That means the skateboard has less momentum.

Momentum affects how difficult it is to stop a moving object. For example, a slow-rolling soccer ball has low speed and low mass. A person can easily stop the ball

A fast-moving train has a lot of momentum, so it is hard to stop.

because it doesn't have much momentum. A fast-moving train has high speed and high mass. It is much harder to stop because it has a lot of momentum.

A moving object keeps its momentum unless a force causes it to change. Sometimes an object is slowed down by the surface it moves across. This can happen because of **friction**.

Think of a hockey puck sliding across ice. There is friction between the puck and the ice. This friction causes the puck to lose momentum. In time, the puck will come to a stop.

A hockey puck loses momentum because of friction between the puck and the ice.

CHAPTER 3

MOMENTUM AND COLLISIONS

Sometimes one object bumps into a second object. This is called a **collision**. During the collision, the two objects **exert** forces on each other. This causes the momentum of each object to change.

Pool balls experience changes in momentum when they collide.

When cars collide, they exchange momentum. This often involves damage to the cars.

If no other forces are acting on the objects, the total momentum stays the same. This means both objects experience the same change in momentum but in **opposite** directions.

For example, think of two objects colliding along a line. Imagine that the first object is in motion. The second object is at rest. Suppose the two objects have the same mass. In this case, the first object will stop. It will give all of its momentum to the second object.

Now suppose the first object is lighter than the second object.

In this case, the first object will bounce backward because of the collision. The second object will move forward.

Finally, suppose the first object is heavier than the second. Again, the second object will move forward. But the first object will keep moving forward, too. It will just be slower. In all three examples, the total momentum stays the same if no other forces are acting on the objects.

HOW COLLISIONS AFFECT MOMENTUM

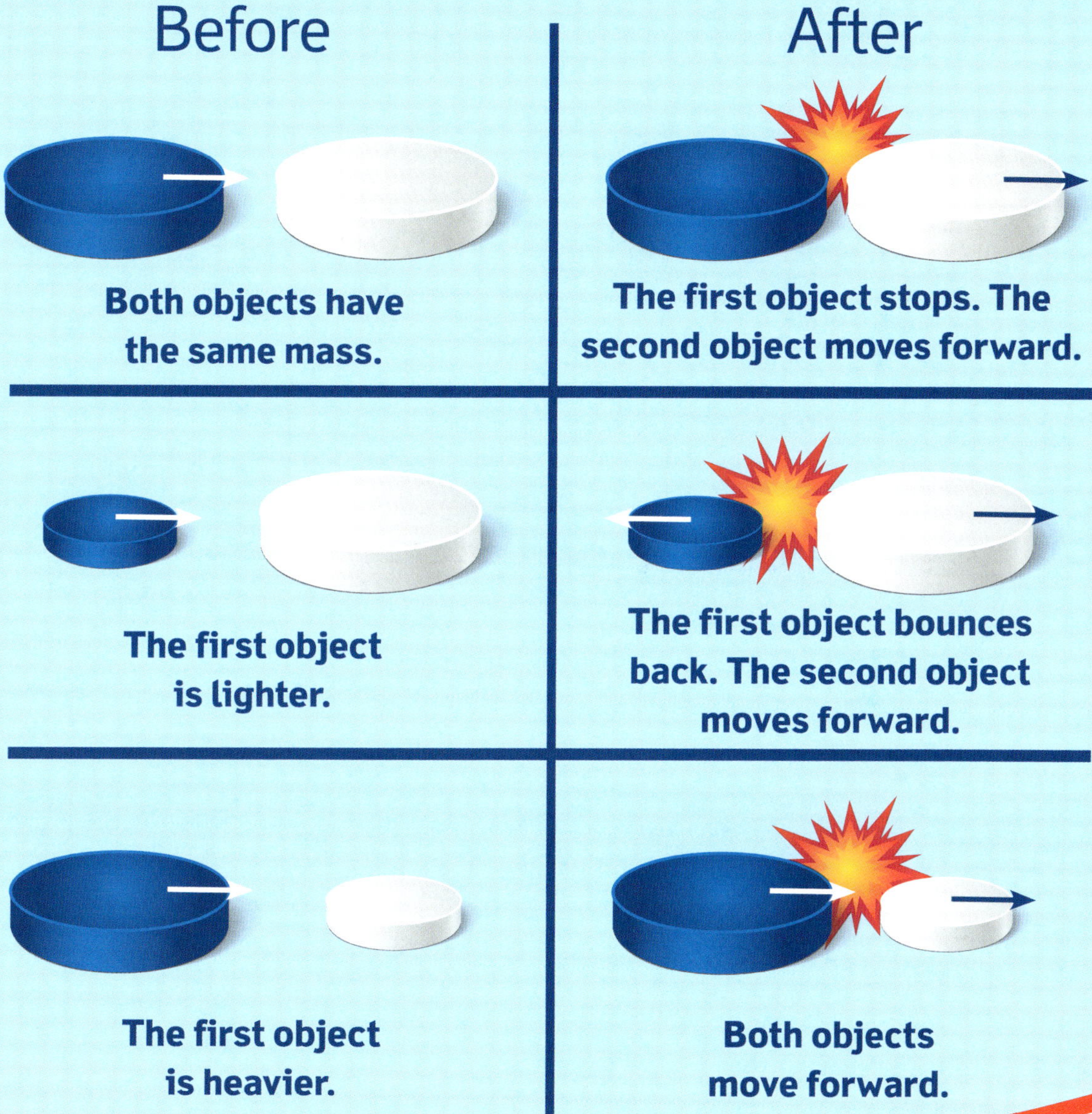

Momentum is important in many activities that people enjoy. For example, all sports involve people or objects moving. That means all sports involve momentum.

Hitting a baseball causes the ball's momentum to change. The ball's mass does not change. But after the ball is hit, it leaves the bat in a different direction. If the speed or direction of the ball changes, the momentum changes.

A ball's momentum changes after it is hit.

In football, a large player running fast has lots of momentum. A small player running slowly has much less momentum. This is why it's harder to tackle the large player running fast. That player has more momentum, so it is harder to get that player to stop.

Momentum is an important part of our lives. Anytime you are moving, think about momentum!

Like all sports, basketball involves momentum.

SCIENCE IN ACTION!

MOMENTUM WITH SCOOTER BOARDS

How does momentum depend on mass and velocity? Do this experiment to find out.

Step 1: Get two identical scooter boards. Also, gather a group of friends.

Step 2: Choose two friends with approximately the same weight. Have them sit on the scooters near each other.

Step 3: One friend should use his or her feet to push the scooters apart. Do the two scooters move away at about the same speed? Or is one moving faster than the other? Does it matter which friend does the pushing?

Momentum depends in part on each person's mass.

Step 4: Now repeat this experiment with different friends. A heavier friend should be on one scooter. A lighter friend should be on the other. Do the two scooters move away at about the same speed? Or is one moving faster than the other? If they have different speeds, which friend is moving the fastest?

FOCUS ON

MOMENTUM

Write your answers on a separate piece of paper.

1. Write a short paragraph that explains the main ideas of Chapter 3.
2. Do you think athletes should study momentum? Why or why not?
3. Which object has no momentum?
   - **A.** an object that is speeding up
   - **B.** an object that is slowing down
   - **C.** an object that is not moving
4. What affects the momentum of an object?
   - **A.** the mass and velocity of the object
   - **B.** the height and shape of the object
   - **C.** the place and color of the object

5. What does **experience** mean in this book?

*This means both objects **experience** the same change in momentum but in opposite directions.*

- A. to stop
- B. to go through
- C. to understand

6. What does **tackle** mean in this book?

*This is why it's harder to **tackle** the large player running fast. That player has more momentum, so it is harder to get that player to stop.*

- A. to bring someone to the ground
- B. to help a player run faster
- C. to make something difficult

Answer key on page 32.

GLOSSARY

collision
When two objects come in contact.

exert
To apply or make use of.

friction
A force that happens when two objects rub against each other.

mass
The amount of matter in an object.

motion
Movement.

opposite
Different or reverse.

velocity
The speed of an object and the direction it moves in.

TO LEARN MORE

BOOKS

Kenney, Karen Latchana. *The Science of Race Cars: Studying Forces and Motion*. North Mankato, MN: Abdo Publishing, 2016.

Muldoon, Kathleen M. *Forces and Motion in the Real World*. Minneapolis: Abdo Publishing, 2013.

Rowell, Rebecca. *Forces and Motion through Infographics*. Minneapolis: Lerner Publications, 2014.

NOTE TO EDUCATORS

Visit **www.focusreaders.com** to find lesson plans, activities, links, and other resources related to this title.

INDEX

Answer Key: 1. Answers will vary; **2.** Answers will vary; **3.** C; **4.** A; **5.** B; **6.** A